WAN2TLK?

ltle bk
of txt
ms

WAN2TLK?

ltle bk of txt msgs

First published in Great Britain in 2000 by
Michael O'Mara Books Limited
9 Lion Yard
Tremadoc Road
London SW4 7NQ

A CIP catalogue record for this book is available from the British Library

Papers used by Michael O'Mara Books Limited are natural, recyclable
products made from wood grown in sustainable forests. The manufactur
processes conform to the environmental regulations of the country of or

ISBN 978-1-84317-082-2

10 9 8 7 6

Designed and typeset by Design 23

Printed and bound in Great Britain by William Clowes Ltd, Beccles, S

CONTENTS

INTRODUCTION

Text messaging is the smart way to communicate in the 21st Century. Everyone, men and women, young and old use it, but especially the young, and it has become the fastest growing service on every network. Why?

Perhaps it is because it's discreet. You can set your phone to vibrate rather than ring when you receive a message and you don't cause a nuisance to others when you reply! We don't recommend it of course, but I understand from teachers that it has replaced passing notes in class as a way of expressing those irresistible asides or making plans for after school. It's cheaper than calling, so you don't use up precious call time as quickly – a boon to 'pay as you go' users especially. It is an international service, so that you can communicate when you are abroad without having to buy extra cards or adaptations for your phone and all at local rates.

All very sensible reasons to join the communication revolution. But if you are still unconvinced, you might like to know that it is also great fun. You can learn and contribute to a whole new language, created by the users. Surveys show that men find it especially tempting to express their feelings by text messaging, especially those tricky ones like 'I love you' and 'I'm sorry!' Young people use it to finalize their infinitely flexible plans and text messaging is a great way to introduce yourself to a stranger at a noisy club or party. Members of the Muslim community in the UK have even used it to call the faithful to prayer. Text messaging has its own grammar and 'netiquette' developed from e-mail and Internet chat rooms, so don't use capital letters – it is classed as shouting and considered very rude! That is unless it stands for a new word or a double letter!

WAN2TLK? contains all the information you need to start chatting, with over 1250 abbreviations and 'emoticons' and their meanings. So just go to the messages option 'write messages' on your phone and start to type. It will guess what you are trying to say, or you can press the options menu and insert words, numbers or symbols – then send. This little phrase book will make you an expert in no time and you can use it for Internet communication too. Welcome to their world.

WAN2TLK?

Basic emoticons

Chatting to old friends and making new ones on your mobile 'phone, or on the internet can be the best and cheapest way to make plans, have a row, start a romance or end an affair and it's discreet! But your messages can be open to misinterpretation when the person you are talking to can't see you or hear the inflection in your voice. The mood of your message is one of the hardest things to convey 'Emoticons' are a shorthand way of explaining or elaborating on your meaning. Made from punctuation marks on your keypad, they take up very little space, can be keyed in seconds and may make the difference between a lasting friendship and social disaster.

The basic smiley face is just a colon, a dash and a close bracket **:-)** and yet when you rotate it through 90° it becomes a smile. Most emoticons rotate through 90° although some are front facing. The sub-text of your words, acronyms or abbreviations will become crystal clear to anyone reading them if you punctuate your message with emoticons, whenever and wherever you feel like it. Emoticons can also be used just for fun, and a lot of creativity goes into making pictures and jokes using the minimum number of characters. The examples below are the basic emoticons in use. You will find even shorter versions, jokes and pictures as well as acronyms and abbreviations in the pages that follow. **HAND :-) !!**

Emoticon	Meaning
;-) ;) ;->	winking happy faces; for comments said tongue-in-cheek
:-(:(:-<	sad, disappointed faces
:-p :-P	faces with tongues stuck out at you
:-]	I am very jolly
:-[	I am down and unhappy
:-D	I am very happy
:-I	I couldn't care less
8-) 8) B-) B)	smiling faces from someone who wears glasses or sun glasses, or has a wide-eyed look

>:-)	a devil with a grin; for those devilish remarks
O:-)	an angel with a halo; for those innocent remarks
<:-)	wearing a dunce's cap; for those stupid questions.
m(_ _)m	deep bow used for apologizing or expressing thanks (viewed from the front)
*^_^*	a huge dazzling grin
:-)	I'm joking
;-)	I have just made a flirtatious and/or sarcastic remark "don't hit me for what I just said"
:-(	I did not like that last

	statement or I am upset or depressed about something
:->	I have just made a really biting sarcastic remark
>:->	I have just made a really devilish remark
>;->	I have just made a very lewd remark
:-\	I am confused/undecided/ doubtful
:-Q	I have no idea what you are talking about
:-S	words fail me
:-@	I am shocked/screaming
:-O	I am surprised/ yelling or ("uh

oh!")	
:->>	a huge smile
l-(l-)	I am very tired
-text	Underline text
TEXT	YELLING

WAN2TLKFST?
Abbreviations and acronyms for fast talkers

AAM	as a matter of fact
AB	ah bless!
AFAIC	as far as I'm concerned
AFAIK	as far as I know
AKA	also known as
ASAP	as soon as possible
ATB	all the best
B	be
BCNU	be seeing you

Bwd	backward
B4	before
BBFN	bye bye for now
BFN	bye for now
BRB	be right back
BTW	by the way
BYKT	but you knew that
C	see
CMIIW	correct me if I'm wrong
CU	see you
CYA	see you

CUL8R	see you later
CW2CU	can't wait to see you
D/	do
Doin	doing
D	don't
EOL	end of lecture
FAQ	frequently asked question(s)
FITB	fill in the blank
F2T	free to talk
Fwd	forward
FWIW	for what it's worth

FYI	for your information
Gonna	going to
Gr8	great
GD&R	grinning, ducking and running (after snide remark)
GG	good game
HAND	have a nice day
H8	hate
HTH	hope this/to help(s)
Hot4U	hot for you
IAC	in any case
IAE	in any event

IANAL	I am not a lawyer (but...)
ICCL	I couldn't care less
ICL	in Christian love
IDK	I don't know
IYSS	if you say so
IHTFP	I have truly found paradise (or: I hate this f'n place)
IIRC	if I recall correctly
ILUVU	I love you
ILUVUMED	I love you more each day
IMCO	in my considered opinion
IMHO	in my humble opinion

IMNSHO	in my not so humble opinion
IMO	in my opinion
IOW	in other words
ITYFIR	I think you'll find I'm right
IUTLUVUBIAON	I used to love you but it's all over now
IYDKIDKWD	if you don't know I don't know who does
IYKWIM	if you know what I mean
IYKWIMAITYD	if you know what I mean and I think you do
JM2p	just my 2 pennyworth
KIT	keep in touch

L8	late
L8r	later
Luv	love
LOL	lots of luck or laughing out loud
MGB	may God bless
MHOTY	my hat's off to you
MMD	make my day
MMDP	make my day punk!
Mob	mobile
Msg	message
MYOB	mind your own business

NE	any
NE1	anyone
NO1	no one
NRN	no reply necessary
OIC	oh, I see
OTOH	on the other hand
PAL	parents are listening
PCM	please call me
PITA	pain in the ass
PLS	please
PPL	people

PS	post script
R	are
ROF	rolling on the floor
ROFL	rolling on the floor laughing
ROTFL	rolling on the floor laughing
RSN	really soon now
RU	are you?
RUOK?	are you OK?
SITD	still in the dark
SIT	stay in touch
SMS	short message service

SOHF	sense of humour failure
SOME1	someone
Stra	stray
SWG	scientific wild guess
SWALK	sealed with a loving kiss
THNQ	thank you
Thx	thanks
TIA	thanks in advance
TIC	tongue in cheek
TI2GO	time to go
TPTB	the powers that be

TTFN	ta ta for now
TTUL	talk to you later
TWIMC	to whom it may concern
TUVM	thank you very much
U	you
UR	you are
WAN2	want to
WAN2TLK?	want to talk?
W/	with
W	without
Wknd	weekend

WRT	with respect to
WTTW	word to the wise
WUCIWUG	what you see is what you get
X	kiss
Xoxoxoxo	hugs and kisses
YKWYCD	you know what you can do
YMMV	your mileage may vary (you may not have the same luck I did)
YR	your
YTLKIN2ME?	you talking to me?
YWIA	you're welcome in advance
YYSSW	yeah, yeah, sure, sure, whatever

1	one
2	to, too
2day	today
2moro	tomorrow
2nlt	tonight
3sum	threesome
4	for
<G	grinning
<J>	joking
<L>	laughing
<O>	shouting
<S>	smiling
<Y>	yawning

YYSSW
Yeah, Yeah, Sure, Sure, Whatever!
Tell me how you really feel

:-)	ha ha
l-)	hee hee
l-D	ho ho
:->	hey hey
:-(	boo hoo
:-l	hmmm
:-O	oops
:-*	ooops
:-o	uh oh!

{}	'no comment'
I:-O	no explanation given
:-o	oh, no!
#:-o	oh, no!
:-0	ohhhhhh!
I:-O	big ohhhhhh!
<:-O	eeek!
O:-)	for those innocent souls
%+{	from the loser of a fight
<:-)	for dumb questions
:-)))	reeeaaaalllly happy
;-) or P-)	wink, wink, nudge, nudge

:-P	nyahhhh!
:-7	that was a wry remark
*8=(:	I am a blithering idiot
>;-('	I am spitting mad
:-)~	I am drooling (in anticipation)
:-9	I am licking my lips
(-:	I am left-handed
:'-(	I am crying
<3	I love you
:'-)	I am so happy, I am crying
:~-(	I am bawling

:-@	I am screaming
:-&	I feel tongue-tied
:*(@)	I am drunk and shouting
<&-I	I feel foolish and tearful
((H)))	a big hug
:-X	a big wet kiss
(:-D	I can't keep a secret or you are a blabber mouth
:-S	my last message didn't make sense
:-D	I am laughing (at you!)
I-O	I am bored/yawning/snoring

:-o zz z z Z Z	I am bored
:^U	I turn my face away
:^Y	I turn my poker face away
:-X	my lips are sealed
:-#	my lips are still sealed
:-C	I am really bummed
:-/	I am sceptical
:-T	I am keeping a straight face
o'!	I am feeling pretty grim (profile)
o'"	I am pursing my lips (profile)
o'J	smiling (profile)

o'P	sticking tongue out (profile)
o'r	sticking tongue out (profile)
o'T	keeping a straight face (profile)
o'U	yawning (profile)
o'V	shouting (profile)
o'Y	whistling (profile)
o'	frowning (profile)
o'v	talking (profile)
o'w	lying (profile)
7=^>	I am happy (3/4 view)
:-S	I am confused
:*(	I am crying softly

:-@!	I am cursing
:-"	whistling casually
:-e	I am disappointed
(:-...	I am heart-broken
:-t	I am cross and pouting
I-I	I am going to sleep
:*)	I am drunk
%-)	I am drunk but happy
L	I am blotto (sideways)
:*)?	are you drunk?
:#)	I am drunk every night

%*@:-(	I am hungover with a headache
%-<I>	I am drunk with laughter
:-W	I am lying (forked tongue)
:^)	I have personality
d :-)	hats off to your great idea
:-(*)	that comment made me sick
(><)	I am anally retentive
(@ @)	You're kidding!
(:-IK-	this is a formal message
(-_-)	this is my secret smile
@*&$!%	you know what that means...

(O—<	I suspect something fishy is going on
-/-	I am stirring up trouble
**-(	I am very, very shocked
:^D	great! I like it!
M:-)	I salute you (respect)
:-$	put your money where your mouth is
:+(	I am hurt by that remark
:~(	I'm feeling put out
>-COD	I am "floundering" for something to say
/O\	I am ducking

.^,	I am looking sideways/happy
:-L	I am blank with cigarette or pipe
=-o	I am surprised
<=-O	I am frightened
=-<>	I am awe struck
)I-[	I am tired and grumpy and very unhappy
(]:-)	I am gung ho
$->	I am happily excited
I-o	I am squinting while talking
:~(~~~	I am moved to tears
O-(==<	I am chastised and/or chagrined

__.	I am properly chastised and/or chagrined
__/~`-'~_/	I don't follow your line of thought
I-{	"Good Grief!" (Charlie Brown?)
===:[OO']>:===	I have been railroaded
=^)	I am open minded
\o/	PTL (praise the lord, or pass the loot?) (sideways)
B-D	"Serves you right, dummy!!"
>w	oh really! (ironic)
8-]	"wow, maaan"
OO	Please read now (headlights on msg)

O-G-<	me, me, me (pointing to self (midget whole body)
O-S-<	I am in a hurry (midget whole body)
O-Z-<	in a big hurry (midget whole body)

WUCIWUG?
What you see is what you get
So what do you look like really?

]-I	I am wearing sunglasses
B:-)	I am wearing sunglasses on my head (cool)
B-I	I am wearing cheap sunglasses
::-)	I am wearing normal glasses
g-)	I am wearing pince-nez glasses
V^J	with glasses, seen from the left side (portrait, talking)
(-E:	I am wearing bifocals
B-)	I am wearing horn-rimmed glasses

R-)	I am wearing broken glasses
l-(	I have lost my contact lenses
@:-)	I am wearing a turban
:-)8	I am well dressed
:-)-8	I am a big girl
B*)	I have a moustache and designer sunglasses!
:-{)	I have a moustache
:-3	I have a handlebar moustache
:-=)	I am an older man/woman with a moustache
:-#l	I have a bushy moustache

`(:-{~`	I am bearded
`:-)##`	I am seriously bearded
`:-)}`	I have a goatee beard
`:^{}>`	I have a moustache and beard
`(8-{)}`	I am bearded with a moustache and glasses
`I:-)`	I have a monobrow
`/;-)`	I have a cockeyed monobrow
`` `:-) ``	I shaved one of my eyebrows off this morning
`,.'v`	I have short hair (profile)
`,o'v`	I have short hair (profile)
`=o'v`	I have a mohawk (profile)

~o'v	I have a long fringe (profile)
?:-)	I have wavy hair, parted on right
}:-)	my hair is parted in the middle in an updraft
(-)	I need a haircut
@:-}	I am just back from the hairdresser
~:-P	I am thinking and steaming having only one single hair
{:-)	I am wearing a toupee
;:-)	I am wearing a really bad toupee
}:-(	my toupee is at risk from a high wind

r:-)	I have a ponytail
@:-)	I have wavy hair
#:-)	I have tangled hair
&:-)	I have curly hair
@.'v	I have curly hair (profile)
?:)	I have a single curl of hair
{:-{)}	I have a new hair style, moustache and beard
:-(>~	I just washed my goatee, and I can't do a thing with it
/8^{~	I have a lopsided hair line, glasses, moustache, and goatee
&:-]	I am very handsome with square jaw

&8-]	I too am very handsome, also with square jaw
:-~)	I have a cold
:x(	I habe a code in by dose
:-R	I have the flu
:%)%	I have acne
:-))	I have a double chin
:-#	I wear braces
:-{#}	I am wearing braces too
H-)	I am cross-eyed
:^)	I have a broken nose
:v)	I have a broken nose, but the other way

`}:^#)`	I have a pointy nose
`o^v`	I have a pointy nose (profile)
`:=)`	I have two noses
`?-(`	I have a black eye
`:<)`	I am a public school student
`I-I`	this is me asleep
`(-.-)Zzz...`	this is me sleeping (sideways)
`(,'%/)`	I have slept too long on one side
`#(,'%/)`	I have slept too long on one side and didn't have time to wash my hair
`*<8-)X`	I am wearing a party outfit with hat and bow-tie

{}-8]	I am left-handed and bearded with glasses and headphones
do'v	I am wearing a hard hat (profile)
(:-)}	I am bald and bearded
:-{}	I am wearing lipstick
:-+	I may be wearing too much lipstick
:-) ,	I have an outie belly button
:-) .	I have an innie belly button

GET REAL! VITAL INFO

:-Q	I smoke
:-"	I am a heavy smoker
:/i	no smoking
(^^)y-~~~	I am smoking now (sideways)
:-j	I am smoking and smiling
:Ui	I am smoking as we speak
:Uj	I am smoking and smiling as we speak
:-?	I smoke a pipe
:-`	I am spitting out my chewing tobacco

:-[	I am a vampire
:-E	I am a bucktoothed vampire
+-:-)	I am the Pope (or other religious leader)
-:-)	I am a punk rocker
-:-(	real punk rockers don't smile
:-) ... :-(... :-) ... :-(	I have mood swings
O-)	I am a scuba diver
:%)	I am an accountant
:?)	I am a philosopher
L:-)	I have just graduated
C:-)	I am modest with a large brain capacity

&;-P	I am a suave guy on the make
{{-}}}	I'm a refugee from the '60's
(:-) ?	I am having a sex change
***:-} 8 8-**	I am a transvestite
:-) : 8-^-	I need some corrective surgery
:-\ : 8o	I have just had a cold shower
:-)K-	I am wearing a shirt and tie
={:-)]	the answer wasn't in the bottle
***8-I**	I am a nerd
!8-)	I am a nerd with combed hair
***X-I**	I am a dead nerd

:-)I	I'm going out on the town
~:o	I am a baby
~:@	I am a baby with a dummy
>[:^)	I watch too much TV
!#!^*&~ >:-(	I am very angry after losing hours of work
+<#^v	I am your knight in shining armour (profile)
#!^~/	I am kissing and wearing shades (profile)
*<o'v	I am wearing a bobble cap (profile)
l:/	I am constipated

O :-)	I am an angel (at heart, at least)
<I-)	I am Chinese
<I-(	I am Chinese and I don't like these kind of jokes
:-)*	I speak Esperanto
C=:-)	I am a chef
*<:-)	I am wearing a Santa Claus hat
3:]	I have a pet like this
3:[	my pet is vicious
E-:-)	I am a ham radio operator
%-6	I am braindead

[:-)	I am wearing a walkman
d:-)	I am wearing a baseball cap
q:-)	I am wearing a baseball cap backwards
(:I	I am an egghead
<:-I	I am a dunce
:-0	I'm not deaf (Quiet please)
.-)	I have only one eye
,-)	ditto...but I'm winking
X-(	I have just died
8 :-)	I am a wizard
:-)^<	I am a big boy

:-)8<	I am a big girl
:-]	I am a blockhead
:-}X	I wear a bow-tie
!#!^*&:-)	I am in two minds
<!==!)	I have a car
.—...	I am an ABBA fan

MDGTMSGES
Even shorter shorthand

A lot of these can be typed without noses to make midget messages for really fast communication.

:)	happy
:]	friendly
=)	friendly 2
:}	what?
:>	what?
:@	what?
:C	what?

:Q	what?
:D	laughter
:) :) :)	loud guffaw
:I	hmmm...
;)	smirking
:(	sad
:[	real downer
; (	chin up
:O	yelling
:V	shouting
:c	really unhappy

:C	unbelieving
:/)	not funny
:?	licking lips
:~)	yummee
:8	talking out both sides of your mouth
:,(	crying
:Y	a quiet aside
;?	wry remark, tongue-in-cheek
;}	leer
:I :-	déjà vu
::=))	double vision

[!]	hug
[]	hugs and ...
:*	kisses
I*	kiss (eyes closed)
:-	male
>-	female
: t	pouting
II	asleep
^o	snoring
&l	that made me cry
:k	biting my lip

:]	biting sarcasm
:-q	trying to touch tongue to nose
'!	(profile) grim
""	(profile) pursing lips
'J	(profile) smiling
'P	(profile) sticking tongue out
'T	(profile) keeping a straight face
'U	(profile) yawning
'V	(profile) shouting
'Y	(profile) whistling
'\	(profile) frowning

oo-	puzzled, confused
'r	(profile) sticking tongue out
'v	(profile) talking
'w	(profile) speaking with forked tongue
:")	embarrassed
__!	enough for now
:!	foot in mouth
8O	omigod!
:@	it's true, I swear
X-(	mad
>:-<	mad

&l	makes me cry
:(*)	makes me sick
:-S	makes no sense
o/	excuse me, not waving but drowning
lP	yuk
8	infinity
:-8(	condescending stare
8-l	suspense
^^	happiness (Japanese symbol)
^^;	embarrassment (Japanese symbol)

`;;`	sadness (Japanese symbol)
`||*)`	handshake accepted (taking)
`M-),:X),:-M`	sees no evil, hears no evil, speaks no evil
`8-S`	sees all evil
`O+`	for women's messages
`^L^`	happy (sideways)
`^(^`	happy variation (sideways)
`^)^ ^(^`	two people talking (sideways)
`i-=<***i`	CAUTION: has flame thrower
`i-=<*** __.`	CAUTION: has flame thrower and uses it!

i-=<****** o-(==<	CAUTION: has flame thrower and uses it!
o=	a burning candle for flames (shouting messages of an unpleasant nature)
-=	a doused candle to end a flame
..._ _ _ ...	S.O.S.
O>-<l=	messages of interest to women
O-&-<	I'm doing nothing (has arms crossed) (mini whole body)
:————)	you are a big liar

WAN2CAPIC?
Want to see a picture?

@>—;—	rose
O:-)	angel
0*-)	angel winking
:= I	baboon
`AR~	baby elephant (sideways)
(:=	beaver
pq`#'	bull (sideways)
=:)	bunny
=:x	another bunny
}I{	butterfly

`})i({`	butterfly – an even prettier one
`~M`'~`	camel (sideways)
`}:-X`	cat
`` `' ``	cat's eyes in the night
`__Λo_`	caterpillar
`8^`	chicken
`3:-o`	cow
`pp#`	cow (sideways)
`:3-]`	dog
`]B=8}`	dragon
`.V`	duck

(:<>	another duck
#B<>	duck, with a spike haircut & Ray-Bans, quacking
6V)	elephant
<:3	ferret
>-^);>	fish
><FISH>	fish
>-",",",",",-)D>	fish
9)	frog
>^,,^	kitty cat
@(*0*)@	koala bear
<:3)~~~~	mouse

~\\ (^o^) /~/~	octopus (Japanese symbol)
:=)	orangutan
:8)	pig
3:[	pitbull
~~8}	snake
∧o∧	spider
<:>==	turkey
(	unhappy Cheshire cat
'~;E	unspecified 4-legged creature
:<=	walrus
:V	woodpecker

WAN2CMORE?

_:^)	American Indian
>>>>>:========	(asparagus)
C=:-)	chef
~:	child
*<l<l<l=	Christmas tree
*<):o)	clown
*-=l8-D	clown
*(H	downhill skier
((Y))	fat lady
(((Y)))	fatter lady
(..(Y)..)	fattest lady

:)))	fat man
C:#	football player
/:-)	Frenchman with a beret
(D:-]	general
-(:-)	German soldier from WWI
oO:)&	grandmother
>:^(	headhunter (Amazon style)
l^o	hepcat
]:)l—<	king
+<ll-)	knight
'v	knight (profile)
\.^./	lotus position, seen from above

{:-) 8 > <	mermaid
^v^v^	mountains
∧_∧	mountain range
):-(	Nordic
P-(	pirate
lc:()	pygmy with bone in hair
8x	scissors
*l:^)(.)(...)	snowman
>[l	television
#:o\:o/:o\:o/:oll	totem pole
-=#:-)	wizard
<*(:-?	a wizard who doesn't know the answer

WAN2SPTA*?
Famous for 15 seconds

: =)	Adolf Hitler
{:^=(	Adolf Hitler
{	Alfred Hitchcock
:-)==	Arnold Schwarzenegger
#:o+=	Betty Boop
&:-o-8-<	Betty Boop
:'O	Bob Hope
>8o!...	Bugs Bunny with carrot
IIII8^)X	Cat in the Hat

((: =)X	Charlie Chaplin
CI:-=	Charlie Chaplin
:/7)	Cyrano de Bergerac
{:<>	Daffy Duck
C8<]	Darth Vader
(8=X	Death (Mr. Death to you) (skull & X bones)
:-8p	Dizzy Gillespie (puffed cheeks and trumpet)
:-) 8	Dolly Parton
:$)	Donald Trump
5:-)	Elvis

@:)	Elvis
EK(	Frankenstein
[:=I]	Frankenstein's monster
`,`,`,`,`:I	Mrs. Frankenstein's monster
:^{=	Frank Zappa
7:-)	Fred Flintstone
>>-O->	General Custer
I:['	Groucho Marx
(:^(	Jack Nicholson in Chinatown
?:^[]	Jim Carrey
:(=)	Jimmy Carter

:###)	Jimmy Durante
(8 {	John Lennon
:-.)	Madonna, Marilyn Monroe
8(:-)	Mickey Mouse
/\\/:\\	The Mummy
(Z(:^P	Napoleon
:—)	Pinocchio
:'}	Richard Nixon
3:*>	Rudolph the reindeer
*<l:-)	Santa Claus
)-:l<*	Sanity Clause
:-) :-) :-) :-)	Shirley MacLaine

3 :-)	Bart Simpson
{8->	Bart Simpson
(_8^(l)	Homer Simpson
(_8(l)	Homer Simpson
@@@@:-)	Marge Simpson
{8-*	Maggie Simpson
{8-)	Lisa Simpson
B-(8	Sir Robin Day
:_(	Van Gogh
...(	Wile E. Coyote after attempt on road runner's life
=IB-{I###	ZZ Top

WAN2PLA?
Want to play? –
Far-fetched and fantasy

:—(Message about/from someone sad because he or she has a large nose

:-D*   I am laughing so hard that I did not notice that a 5-legged spider is hanging from my lip

>8-O-(&)   Message about/from someone who has just realized that they have a tapeworm

~oE]:-l   Fisherperson heading for market with a basket on his or her head containing a three-legged octopus that is giving off smell rays

>:-[-{9	Person who is none too pleased to be giving birth to a squirrel
}:^#})	I am happy though my toupee is being blown upwards and I have a bushy moustache, a pointy nose and a double chin
+-(	I have been shot between the eyes
(X0ll)	Double hamburger with lettuce and tomato please
(: (=l	Message about/from someone wearing a ghost costume (mini whole body)
(-o-)	Imperial Tie Fighter ("Star Wars")
;-)}</////>	Corporate-type guy

&B-]}</////>	A corporate-type with aviator glasses, wavy hair & tie
:-)-O	Smiling doctor with stethoscope
*;-~i	A lady replying to a guy by closing both eyes & puffing nonchalantly on her cigarette
(:>-<	A thief: hands up! (mini whole body)
:-) >=>	Message about/from someone reading a book
>]}	Message about/from a dragon wearing sunglasses
{:-I 8( )>	You are going to be a father!

>:-(8 >	Message about/from a female after reading sexist opinions on feminists
@O=E<=	Message about/from a woman in a skirt wearing a turtleneck sweater (mini whole body)
B-)-[<	Message about/from a man wearing sunglasses and swimming trunks (mini whole body)
o>8<l=	Messages about/to interesting women (mini whole body)
:-)</////>	Message from/about a guy with a bad tie on
<\\\\>(-:	Message from/about a left-handed guy with a bad tie on

::-bld-::	Message about/from a person wearing glasses and sticking out tongue at mirror
:-) (-: + :-o o-: + :-Pd-:	a kissing (sequence)
@ @B-)	Message about/from a bouffant woman with catseye frame glasses
<<<<(:-)	Message from a hat salesman
<&&>	Message concerning rubber chickens
>< ><	Message about/to someone wearing argyle socks
<{:-)}	Message in a bottle
<:-)<<l	Message from a space rocket

?-(	Message about someone with a black eye
:	Message about fuzzy things
*:**	Message about fuzzy things with fuzzy moustaches
%-)	Message about people with broken glasses
(:-)	Message dealing with bicycle helmets
(:-$	Message indicating person is ill-informed about the Renaissance
<@:{(>X	Message about/from a moustached Chinese man with a toupee, goatee and bow tie

2B|^2B	Message about Shakespeare
OO	A guy is mooning you
O:O	A girl is mooning you
:-))-:	Masking theatrical comments
C=>8*)	Message about/from devilish chef with glasses and a moustache
C=}>;*{O)	Message about/from a drunk, devilish chef with a toupee in an updraft, a moustache, and a double chin
}:~#})	Message about/ from a bushy-moustached ugly-nosed man or woman with a double-chin

I-Q	Message about/from a Chinese person smoking and yelling
-:	Message about/from someone upside down with a brick in his mouth
@&o/	Message about/from a tearful-sceptic, wearing a turban
{I^x~	Message about/ from someone with hair-parted-in-the-middle, kissing and drooling
<X	Message about/from someone crazy and giving a wet kiss
+-::(@)	Message about/from a religious wearing normal glasses but shouting

<,-?	Message about/from someone with one-winking-eye-only and smoking a pipe
<&*c	Message about/from someone tearful, drunk and unhappy
>&-r	Message about/from someone tearful and sticking tongue out
{:0	Message about/from orator wearing a toupee
}::-?	Message about/from someone wearing a toupee in an updraft, wearing normal glasses and smoking a pipe
B:*/	Message about/from someone drunk and undecided with sunglasses on head

*^O	Message about/from a crazy-big-mouth
<:@0	Message about/from a pig-nosed orator
<8-~)	Message about/from a swimmer with a cold and smiling
>|*b	Message about/from a drunk sticking the tongue out
@0-(	Message about/from a sad scuba-diver wearing a turban
(B:o#	Message about/from an egg-head with sunglasses on head and wearing braces
(8*<	Message from/about an egg-head-swimmer, drunk and mad

*.-)	Message about/from someone one-eyed but smiling
~~0{	Message about/from a burning scuba-diver with a moustache
OOOOBc~	Marge Simpson, unhappy, wearing glasses and drooling
OOOO:@[	pig-nosed -Marge Simpson-vampire
OOOO-{I	Marge Simpson-crazy person with a moustache
OOOOX-~(	dead-Marge Simpson-sad and with a cold
<:-@ 8-	Message about/from a male screaming
<:-) >-	Message about/from a female smiling

[B--~[	Message about/from a vampire wearing a walkman, glasses and with a cold
***!#^!*,-{**	Message about/from a dreamer, one-winking-eye-only and undecided with a moustache
*!#^!*lo#	Message about/from a dreamer wearing braces
!#^!:@)	Message about/from a pig-nosed, smiling dreamer
!#^!:@[	Message about/from a pig-nosed confused vampire
*!#^!*loO	Message about/from a big-mouthed dreamer snoring

!#^!:-)	Message about/from a dreamer, smiling
*(	Message about/from someone crazy and frowning
>8-<	Message about/from someone devilish, surprised and mad
::-{}	Message about/from someone wearing normal glasses and wearing lipstick
@::-x	Message about/from someone wearing a turban, normal glasses and kissing
@,^V	Message about/from someone with one-winking-eye-only, wearing a turban and shouting

<8-{D	Message about/from someone happy, wearing sunglasses and with a moustache
@8[	Message about/from a surprised vampire wearing a turban
<B:-/~	Message about/from someone undecided with sunglasses on head and drooling
[8*l	Message about/from someone drunk with a walkman and wearing sunglasses
@:-v	Message about/from someone wearing a turban and speakin
<B-~D	Message about/from someone happy, wearing glasses and with a cold

`<8*p`	Message about/from someone surprised, drunk and sticking tongue out
`<8-{l`	Message about/from a foolish swimmer with a moustache
`*<:{`	Message about/from someone with a moustache and wearing a Santa Claus hat
`@:*&`	Message about/from someone drunk, tongue-tied and wearing a turban
`+-X-(`	Message about/from someone dead, religious and frowning
`@.-(@)`	Message about/from someone with one-eye-only wearing a turban and shouting

@B-O~	Message about/from someone with a big mouth wearing a turban, glasses and drooling
<B:^b	Message about/from someone with sunglasses on head and sticking the tongue out
<0-)	Message about/from a scuba-diver, smiling
{B-	Message about/from someone with hair-parted-in-the-middle, sceptical, with glasses
<8r	Message about/from someone wearing sunglasses and sticking tongue out
{loX	Message about/from someone with lips sealed, wearing a toupee

<8^)	Message about/from a swimmer smiling
87)	cartoon character with a long nose and happy
~87(	cartoon character unhappy that he has only one hair on his head
%87)	cartoon character happy he has his curly hair
87D	cartoon character with a long nose...and VERY happy
87P O>w	cartoon character enjoying eating his ice cream cone
87P`` O>w	cartoon character REALLY enjoying eating his ice cream cone

FULL ON

^_^	<	basic happy (Japanese style)
;_;	|	Crying (Japanese style)
@_@	<	Boggle eyed, or glasses (Japanese style)
(_o_)		kowtowing (bowing) person (Japanese style)
*^_^*		blushing (Japanese style)
^_^;;;		embarrassed; cold sweat (Japanese style)
^^;;;		embarrassed; cold sweat (Japanese style)
`\=o-o=/'		I am wearing glasses

())=(	I am drinking wine
-,-	I am sleepy
-.-	I am sleepy too
(o)(o)	I am a well-endowed female
>[]l	I am watching television
oo---oo-Bo	I am a truck driver
,,,^..^,,,	I am being watched by a cat peeking over a fence
(^o^)	I am joyously singing
(^.^)/	waving hello (Japanese style)
(;.;)/~	waving goodbye (Japanese style)

(>_<)	I am furious
(=_=)~	I am sleepy (Japanese style)
(g_g)	I am sleepy
{{{(>_<)}}}	I am freezing (Japanese style)
(*_*)	I am in love
($_$)	I am being greedy
(x_x)	I may be dead
(u_u)	I am sleeping
(OvO)	I am a nightowl

(^-^)	another smile
<^O^>	I am laughing loudly
(@_@)	I am stunned
(o_o)	I am shocked

$$\text{\$ \$ \$ £ £ £ \$ \$ \$}$$

HelpYaFrens2WinTLoTo

CUOnEzESt	see you on easy street
HerCumTGOdTlms	here come the good times
MAkItHPn	make it happen
MAkTWrldGoRnd	make the world go round
MOvnOnUp	moving on up
MOvnUpMOvnOn	moving up, moving on
MunE\$\$\$£££MunE	money, money, money
PlA2Win	play to win

UWATrctALTWelthUNEdOrDsir

you will attract all the wealth you need or desire

2DAsYaLkEDA

today's your lucky day

UC/GtItIfURELEWan

you can get it if you really want

UC/HavItAL

you can have it all

UGtWotItTAks

you've got what it takes

URAFInanshal-=#:-)

you are a financial wizard

£$: -)))

you are a money magnet

££$$CumsEsilE2YaHnds
money comes easily to
your hands

YaShpIsCuMnIn your ship is coming in

LUVLINS2ATRCTATNSHUN
Love lines to attract attention

AintLuvABtch?   ain't love a bitch?

Aint2Proud2Bg   ain't too proud to beg

ALAlOnAmI   all alone am I

ALINEdIsYaSwEtLuvn
all I need is your sweet loving

AlOn?   alone?

AnAFAr2Rmba?   an affair to remember?

&SoIWLWAt4U   and so I will wait for you

O:-)   angel

BABDnt4getMINo

        baby don't forget my number

BABD\GetHOkdOnME

        baby don't get hooked on me

BABINEdYaLuvn   baby I need your loving

BABURDynamIt   baby you are dynamite

BABWeBeTaTrI2GetIt2gtha

        baby we better try to
        get it together

BAs1?   be as one?

BeGn	begging
Brn2BWld	born to be wild
BrnBABBrn	burn baby burn
ChAngYaMnd	change your mind
ChOsME	choose me
CldItBlmFaLnInLuv?	
	could it be I'm falling in love?
CnITAkUHOmLtleGrl?	
	can I take you home little girl?
C/ThsBLuv?	can this be love?
C\TAkMliisOFaU	can't take my eyes off of you

C/UKikIt?	can you kick it?
C/UPrT?	can you party?
C\WAtAnuvaMinit	can't wait another minute
CumOnHOm	come on home
DArME?	dare me?
DaYaThnkImSxE?	do you think I'm sexy?
DncW/ME?	dance with me?
DntBrngMEDwn	don't bring me down
D\ItMAkUFEIGOd	don't it make you feel good?

D\MAkMEWAt2Lng

don't make me wait too long

D\StndSoClOs2ME

don't stand so close to me

D/It4Luv do it for love

D/UBlvInMgic? do you believe in magic?

D/UFEllIkIFEl? do you feel like I feel?

D/UWanME? do you want me?

D/YaD/YaWan2PlsME?

do you, do you want to please me?

EvrEBoDNEdsSumBoD2Luv

everybody needs somebody to love

FEIsLIkT1stTIm	feels like the first time
FrEYaBoD	free your body
GiMEGiMEGiMEAMnAftaMdnIte	
	gimme, gimme, gimme a man after midnight
GiMESumLuvn	gimme some loving
GivIn2ME	give in to me
GivItUp	give it up
GoNaMAkUnOFaUC\RfUs	
	gonna make you an offer you can't refuse

Got2GetUIn2MlLIf	gotta get you into my life
GtIt2gtha	get it together
GtItWIIUC/	get it while you can
GTnReD4Luv	getting ready for love
HaP2gtha?	happy together?
HAU	hey you
HIdME	hold me
IC/MAkUFElGOd	I can make you feel good
IC\GtNoStisfctn	I can't get no satisfaction

ID\NoILuvdUTLISawURokNRol
> I didn't know I loved you till I saw you rock and roll

IFEILuvCumnOn I feel love coming on

IGotUBAb I got you babe

IJstKEpThnknAboutUBAB
> I just keep thinking about you baby

IJstWan2MAkLuv2U
> I just want to make love to you

ILTAkUHOm2nIt I'll take you home tonight

ImALUNEd	I'm all you need
ImNotInLuv	I'm not in love
ImQulifd2Stsfl	I'm qualified to satisfy
IMSdTBus	I missed the bus
INEdSum1	I need someone
INOWotBysLlk	I know what boys like
IRLEWan2CU2nlt	I really want to see you tonight
IsThsALuvThng?	is this a love thing?
IsntItTIm?	isn't it time?

IWaNaBYaMn	I wanna be your man
IWanUINEdUILuvU	
	I want you, I need you, I love you
IW\NrmLEDoThsKindaThng	
	I wouldn't normally do this kind of thing
JstSANo	just say no
KEpMEInMnd	keep me in mind
LetItBME	let it be me
LetLuvRUl	let love rule
LetMENo	let me know

LetYaLuvFlO	let your love flow
LItMIFIr	light my fire
LOkWotUStrtd	look what you started
LtsGtTTOs	let's get tattoos
LtsSpndTNIt2gtha	let's spend the night together
LuvLIkARckt	love like a rocket
LuvT1URW/	love the one you're with
MABBAB	maybe baby
MadAbtU	mad about you

MadIfUD	mad if you don't
MAd2Luv	made to love
MAkItHPn	make it happen
MAkItREl	make it real
MAkItSOn	make it soon
MakItW/ME	make it with me
MAkLuv2ME	make love to me
MorThnAWmn	more than a woman
MovYaBoD	move your body

NEdU2nIt	need you tonight
NEdYaLuvSoBad	need your love so bad
NETImNEPlAc	any time, any place
NevaFndALuvLIkThsB4	
	never found a love like this before
NEWAThtUWanME	
	any way that you want me
NOLmt	no limit
0ls4eva	nothing is forever
1OfThseNIts?	one of these nights?
OpnYa<3	open your heart

OUPrTThng	oh you pretty thing
PlEsD\Go	please don't go
PSSblyMAB?	possibly maybe?
ReD4Luv?	ready for love?
ReDOrNot	ready or not?
ReD2Go?	ready to go?
RmbaME?	remember me?
ROLW/It	roll with it
RsQmE	rescue me

M:-)	respect
Rn2ME	run to me
RnBABRn	run baby run
RSVP	answer please

RUGeTinEnufOfWotMAksUHaP?
are you getting enough of
what makes you happy?

RULOnsum2Nlt?   are you lonesome tonight?

RUReD4Luv   are you ready for love?

RUStisfld?	are you satisfied?
SAUD\Mnd	say you don't mind
SAULBTher	say you'll be there
SAUSAME	say you say me
SAULStAUntl2moro	
	say you'll stay until tomorrow
SAUWL	say you will
ShIBy	shy boy
SOHreIAm	so here I am

SOS	help
StAW/MEBAB	stay with me baby
StndBIME	stand by me
StsflMISOl	satisfy my soul
SumLIkItHot	some like it hot

SumThng4TWEknd?
something for the weekend?

SumTHngsGoTaHldOfMI<3
something's got a hold of
my heart

| **SwEtTIknGl** | sweet talking guy |

TAkYaTIm	take your time
Tmptd?	tempted?
2nItCldBTNIt	tonight could be the night
UBIOMIMnd	you blow my mind
UGtTLOk	you got the look
WAtn4AGrlLIkU	waiting for a girl like you
WECnWrkItOut	we can work it out
WenWLICUAgn?	when will I see you again?
WerDoWEGOFrmHre?	where do we go from here?
WEvGotItGoinOn	we've got it going on
WamBam?	wham bham?

Wlcum2TPlesurDOm
> welcome to the pleasure dome

WotevaGetsUThruTNIt
> whatever gets you through the night

WotevaUWan   whatever you want

WotRUWAtn4?   what are you waiting for?

WotsItLIk2BBUtifl?
> what's it like to be beautiful?

WotsLuvGot2DoWi/It?
> what's love got to do with it?

WotsYaNAmWotsYaNo?
> what's your name?
> what's your number?

UREvrEThng2ME you are everything to me

URT1 you are the one

UvGotIt you've got it

UvGotMINoYDntUUseIt?
you've got my number,
why don't you use it?

YaBoDsCLin your body's calling

YaMamaWntLIkMe
your mama won't like me

YaTImIsGNaCum your time is gonna come

YuMEYuMEYuME yummy, yummy, yummy

YumYumGivMESum yum,yum give me some

YngFrE&Sngl young, free and single

EvrEDAInEvrEWAURGeTnBeTa&BeTa
Every day in every way....confidence boosters

ActLIkUMEnIt   act like you mean it

BGOd2YaSlf   be good to yourself

BProudBLoudBHerd
    be proud, be loud, be heard

DAr2BDFrnt   dare to be different

**EvrEDAInEvrEWA
URGeTnBeTa&BeTa**
    every day in every way, you
    are getting better and better

GOYaOnWA   go your own way

IBELvInMrcls	I believe in miracles
LIfsACnch	life's a cinch
LItUpYaWrld	light up your world
0CnStpUNow	nothing can stop you now
TAkItEzE	take it easy
TAkItHIr	take it higher
TDcizunIsYas	the decision is yours
ThAAntCEn0Yt	they ain't seen nothing yet
ThrsAWrldOutSIdYaWndO	
	there's a world outside your window

ThsIsIt	this is it
ThsIsTDA	this is the day
TPwrIsYas	the power is yours
TrnUpTPwr	turn up the power
UCnDoItIfUOnlEThnkUCan	you can do it if you only think you can
UCnHavItAL	you can have it all
UFascin8ME	you fascinate me

UGetWUXpctN\WUDsrvXpctTBeST

you get what you expect,
not what you deserve –
expect the best

UHavFAthInYaSlf you have faith in yourself

URAnInspir8shun you are an inspiration

URA*NowActLIk1 you are a star,
now act like one

URFrleSBrAv&Bold

you are fearless, brave
and bold

UROI! you rule!

URSchA* you are such a star

YaConfdnceShwsOnYaFAc
              your confidence shows on
              your face

YaTImHsCum   your time has come

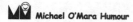

Michael O'Mara Humour

Now you can order other little books direct from Michael O'Mara Books Limited.

The Little Book of Dirty Cockney Rhyming Slang –
        978-1-84317-035-8
The Little Book of Cockney Rhyming Slang –
        978-1-84317-027-3
The Little Book of Crap Advice – 978-1-84317-041-9
The Little Book of Crap Excuses – 978-1-84317-040-2
The Little Book of Farting – 978-1-85479-445-1
The Little Book of Internet Dating – 978-1-84317-173-7
The Little Book of Minge Topiary – 978-1-84317-051-8
The Little Book of Sex Dares – 978-1-84317-194-2

The Little Book of Senior Moments

978-1-84317-255-0

Published April 2008 – £2.50

All Michael O'Mara titles are available by post from:

Bookpost Ltd, PO Box 29, Douglas, Isle of Man IM99 1BQ

Credit cards accepted.

Please telephone: 01624 677237
Fax: 01624 670923
E-mail: bookshop@enterprise.net
Internet: http://www.bookpost.co.uk

Postage and packing is free in the UK.
Overseas customers should allow £2 per book (paperbacks)
and £5 per book (hardbacks).